CHALLENGES OF CHANGE

Adventures in Victorious Senior Living

JIM BLYTHE

Copyright © 2017 by Jim Blythe
Challenges of Change
Adventures in Victorious Senior Living
by Jim Blythe

Printed in the United States of America.

ISBN 9781498495219

All rights reserved solely by the author. The author guarantees all contents are original and do not infringe upon the legal rights of any other person or work. No part of this book may be reproduced in any form without the permission of the author. The views expressed in this book are not necessarily those of the publisher.

Scripture quotations taken from the New King James Version (NKJV). Copyright © 1982 by Thomas Nelson, Inc. Used by permission. All rights reserved.

JamBly163@yahoo.com
Certified Senior Advisor designation info - http://www.csa.us

www.xulonpress.com

Table of Contents

Endorsement vii
Dedication viii
Acknowledgements ix
Introduction xi
My Start in the Mortgage Business 15
The Power of Right-Sizing + Scenarios 20
Fraud & Risk 29
Attitude Determines Altitude 40
Reimagine – Reinvent – Renew 48
Planning for Change: Wills, Powers of
    Attorney, Trusts 55
Mental & Physical Challenges 65
Stay Plugged In 71
Caretakers 74
Power Tools: Plan, Budget, Accomplish 80
Conclusion 89
Resources 91

Jim and Diane,

Thank you for allowing me to read this book that is so vital to the wellbeing and secure living for us in our golden years. It is thorough enough to cover necessary information, understandable enough to be non-threating, organized enough to be easy to follow, and personalized enough to give real life, believable accounts of people just like us.

Dr. Thelma Wells
Founder of Generation Love – Divine Appointment Conferences
Professor, Speaker, Author
www.generationlove.info

Dedication

I would like to dedicate this book to my Dad and Mom, Ed and Jane Blythe, and my Grandparents, Nuel and Isabell Blythe. The lessons they taught me about service, honor, and love have been a constant inspiration to me. We learn best from the examples of others and my family taught me well.

Acknowledgements

I would like to thank my wife Diane for her professional help, guidance, and collaboration to write this book. Without her I could not have completed this work. She is an inspiration, team player, and exceptional editor.

I would also like to thank the Society of Certified Senior Advisors who provided so much training and encouragement to help me work with seniors. I especially want to thank Judy Rough for her help and encouragement. Without Judy and the Society, none of this would have happened.

I want to thank the many seniors I have met with and helped over the last 13 years. Their stories have inspired me and guided me to help others.

Finally I want to thank Thelma Wells for her inspiration and love. She is truly a great teacher, motivator, and lady.

Introduction

To everything there is a season, a time for
every purpose under Heaven ...
Ecclesiastes 3:1

For more than a dozen years now I have been in senior families' homes and listened to their stories in an effort to help them live out their lives with financial success. These are some of the stories I have heard and lived through with families in the heartland of America. Some stories are inspirational and show much vitality and spunk, and some stories are tough to listen to. I have wanted to tell these stories for a long time to help families avoid many of the financial pitfalls I have seen.

Change is the constant throughout life but the older we get the more we resist change until it is forced on us and we have no choice but to do something, and that something is many times difficult. The challenge of change is imagining a new normal. What was familiar and safe will change, because life changes. A spouse passes away or becomes incapable of taking care of themselves. Financial setbacks, medical mishaps, and loss of income can have devastating effects. *Before* the future looks bleak is when we should make a plan and speculate what might need to change. A new "normal" can be a great thing – with planning we can enjoy life and be productive. To do that, we need to be *"proactive"*– *that* is the challenge of change.

When I started my journey as a Reverse Mortgage Specialist, I had a background in finance and real estate, a degree from UT Austin in Finance, and had earned my real estate broker's license while in Austin. I came back to Dallas and became a commercial real estate specialist and ultimately a developer. My forte was my ability to finance properties. In 1994 after several terribly hard years in Dallas' post-savings-and-loan-disaster real estate world, I had to make a living. I was asked to help out with a radio show about real estate and home mortgage finance. That went well and I decided to move into full-time home lending, with an occasional commercial deal on the side to keep things exciting. To learn more about mortgage lending, I became a teacher for a wonderful lady named Nancy Haws. I had a lot to learn, so I taught what I had to learn and made relationships along the way. That worked well for me. I was a natural at figuring out

Introduction

complicated mortgage and title problems. I became the government loan, FHA, and VA "wonder boy."

We began talking about the new reverse mortgage loan for seniors on the air in 2004, and I decided to specialize. My knowledge of FHA and VA really helped. I started the reverse mortgage program for Bank of Oklahoma (in Texas–Bank of Texas). We had eight states in the banking group, and I called on them all. I had a ball helping seniors. In 2007 a friend had recommended I look into getting a Certified Senior Advisor designation to really learn about senior issues. Six months of hard study at night and I was hooked. The material wasn't difficult, but it *was tough* looking into my future: growing *old*. Studying the disturbing issues that arise: Housing, Medical, Care Giving, Legal, Estate, Finance, Psychology ... issue after issue became really painful to read. I passed the exam and became a Certified Senior Advisor in 2007. That's where the story really begins, or should I say stories ... I have loved my career as a Certified Senior Advisor–helping people. I hope these stories help you or someone you love meet the challenges of change.

Jim Blythe, CSA

NMLS 311548   214 502 4600   JamBly163@yahoo.com

My Start in the Mortgage Business

*Though one may be overpowered by another,
two can withstand him.
And a threefold cord is not quickly broken.*
Ecclesiastes 4:12

My career in real estate had been a challenge–that prepared me to advise families about their real estate financial issues. My job in commercial real estate was as a problem solver. I got the tough deals with all kinds of interesting twists and turns and people to work with. When commercial real estate no longer had a place for me after the Savings & Loan disaster of the late 80's, I was fortunate enough to be asked to co-host a radio talk show about real estate and mortgage lending. I jumped in and when offered a job I moved into what I thought would be a better, more rewarding career–a chance to reinvent myself *and* make a living. FHA and VA, both government loans, became my specialty. Not many people wanted to do those loans because of the paperwork involved, but more people needed those loans in order to qualify. Besides, I was a Vietnam Navy Veteran and I wanted to help other veterans. The loans were tougher but rewarding for me, personally. During that time "subprime" became the hot new product, and I quickly saw those loans as disasters looking for places to happen, while FHA and VA loans were still solid. I had many opportunities to turn tough loans into good ones because of the lessons I had learned–to document, document, and document some more.

A realtor came to me with a young lady in tears. She was crying because her credit was so bad she couldn't even rent an apartment, and she and her little girl were forced to live with her parents. The realtor left this lady with me with one of those "lots of luck, brother" looks. So I asked her what had happened. Her boyfriend had stolen her identity, bought a car in her name, taken out a second lien on her condo, and had run up mountains of credit card debt. So when I pulled her credit report it was awful. How had a young woman with a 3 year old gotten in such a mess? There was a foreclosure, a car repo, defaulted credit cards, and a bankruptcy. I asked the next question: Did you report the guy? Thank goodness she had, and he had pled guilty and was convicted.

My Start in the Mortgage Business

I noticed she had three student loans, which had been paid on time throughout this whole firestorm of credit fraud. I had her get the court orders from his conviction and her bankruptcy papers. Her attorney had told her to declare bankruptcy, which made him money but was a huge mistake for her. She was the victim of *FRAUD*.

I took an application and built a file about the size of the Dallas phone book with all the court papers and references as well as the bankruptcy filings and made a time line. The key was the three small student loans she never defaulted on. I went to my first underwriter and she just laughed at me. I learned from my mistake, wrote a summary credit explanation letter, and had the young lady sign it. The second underwriter said no, but she recommended a friend with a well-known lender. I met with the lender and carefully went through the file, asking her advice. I never asked for her approval, just her *advice*. After going through the whole file, as I hoped, the three student loans which were current saved the day. The young lady had loan approval and I had done my first really tough deal. About a month later I was with a date in a restaurant, and the young lady came over to my table and cried and kissed me, and her daughter hugged my leg. I really fell in love with helping people who were in distress. That was 1994. Ten years later I was making a living and enjoying what I was doing.

The key is to know the rules and how to apply them. Chase Bank offered me a job just after the Bank One merger. They recruited me for my FHA and VA skills, and because I had done a few reverse mortgages. A reverse mortgage is a type of FHA/government-insured and regulated loan. I had become very good at FHA loans for new homebuyers, which helped me later learn the reverse mortgage industry.

I went to meeting after meeting and was asked about reverse mortgages. I would summarize them, and then have to say Chase didn't do them. I found that not everyone was a fan of FHA lending. I had four loans declined at Chase and finally called the head of operations and underwriting in Arizona. I asked if they were following the FHA guidelines, or did they make their own. Astonished, she asked me how I got a copy of the guidelines. I had requested it and read it. She reviewed all my files and all were approved within hours. It pays to know what the answer is when you ask the question.

All of this lasted about a year. The senior manager who knew I was dying to do reverse mortgage lending finally called me in and told me that Chase would never do reverse mortgage lending. They wanted me to stay, but if I wanted to go I would get a sterling recommendation. I loved working for Chase and still bank there, but I had to leave in order to do reverse mortgages.

Soon the largest reverse mortgage lender in the nation at that time contacted me, Financial Freedom. They had just approved Bank of Oklahoma and all of its subsidiaries in 8 states. In 2006 I became the only reverse mortgage loan officer in the whole system as a correspondent of Financial Freedom. Now I was on a path to help seniors and make a living. I had also figured out that the crazy subprime-lending atmosphere meant we were headed for a disaster. That was the best decision I could have made.

The Power of Rightsizing

*If any of you lacks wisdom, let him ask of God,
who gives to all liberally and without reproach,
and it will be given to him.*
James 1:5

Everyone wants a dream home, a sanctuary to go to. One of the biggest challenges of change is having the right place to live. Most of the cases I have dealt with not only focus on where to live but how to live. Running out of money is probably one of the biggest fears most seniors have. 95% of the families in retirement have only a small fixed income and their home. What is their biggest expense? Their home. What is the biggest emotional issue? Moving. Almost everywhere I go many questions are raised about senior housing – the key to success is **cash flow**. Changing where we live can be scary … exciting … *both*. Timing really matters. These stories illustrate the profound effect the right home can have on financial and emotional peace of mind.

There is a lot of emotion behind housing change. I remember when I was a kid and my mother and grandmother went to visit friends in the nursing homes in Corsicana. They would come home crying and massively upset. Mother would say to me, "Please Jimmy, never put me in a nursing home." There was and still is an inherent fear for seniors of being moved to a nursing home. Thankfully things are changing for the better in many nursing homes. Even so, understanding that emotional fear of change is important.

How do seniors and families make decisions about housing? That wonderful house you built and raised your family in is probably no longer right for your needs. Do a simple Budget and follow the budget to make a Plan (see Power Tools).

A family in Tulsa found me–the husband had lost his business. They lived in a wonderful home they had built in a very desirable neighborhood. The home was a two-story 3,500 square foot home. When I met with them I noticed it had not been updated in years and needed paint and other touches. Their daughter had been trying to get them to move for years. They had *used all their retirement funds* and were borrowing money from their daughter, who could no longer afford to help them. They wanted to do a reverse mortgage to stay in their home. It was familiar; it was where they had raised their children; it was their *HOME*. The daughter had privately begged me to be the voice of reason. I did a simple budget and there was no way they could afford to stay in their home. The wife was about to turn 62 and had no social security income. His social security income was limited, and an hour of doing the math made it evident. I showed them a plan to sell their home and downsize. Using a reverse mortgage to purchase a home, they could sell their home, buy a new one, put money in the bank, and not have a monthly payment. Their home was their only investment, but also their biggest expense.

Their daughter had recently moved into a condo complex and there was a unit available near her. Their big home went on the market and sold in a week, thanks to a really smart realtor. They bought the condo and we did the reverse for purchase. No monthly payments, and under the new FHA rules she had the rights of survivorship. She was protected in case anything happened to him. I kept telling their daughter that Dad needed to see a doctor because I saw symptoms that told me he had had a mild stroke. The family had a new, much smaller, better home they could afford. They also had about $75,000 in the bank. How great is that? Unfortunately he had another stroke and didn't make it. Turns out the stroke could have been prevented with medication. Nevertheless, his wife was in a home and had money in the bank and would be able to start taking his social security when she turned 62–a bittersweet tale.

I met a family in Colorado. He had had lung cancer and a heart bypass. He was lucky to be alive to say the least. They couldn't stay in Colorado at the altitude they were living. Their son was in Belton, Texas. They sold their home and netted $128,000. They couldn't find anything that fit for that price. A banker friend called and explained the situation. They found a $170,000 home that was perfect. We did the reverse mortgage for purchase and they had over $50,000 in the bank. They are really happy and near their son. No monthly payment and when his issues take their final toll she can stay in the home.

There was another family in Grove, Oklahoma. They had bought their dream home on the Grand Lake of the Cherokees. He had a heart attack and she came down with cancer. They were traveling up and down the turnpike every day to Tulsa and medical facilities. They needed to sell their home to move closer to medical facilities and family. They sold their large home and were able to move into a good home thanks to the reverse for purchase. Medical availability and family made a great difference for them, made easier by the reverse mortgage.

Giving up your family home is hard. I have had too many of those difficult conversations. Once I was with a widower whose wife had recently passed. He lived in a 1915 home in Highland Park–a very exclusive area of Dallas. The home was worth $1,250,000 but was in disrepair with window units. The utility bills were out of sight. He had *borrowed* money to live on because his social security income had been cut by the loss of his wife. He was living on borrowed money and $1,750.00 a month. His utility bills were over $450 per month, but he had a blessing in a home that was worth a fortune. I explained that FHA would not do a reverse mortgage on his home because of all the disrepair factors. He needed to sell and relocate–that home was too much for him, anyway. I showed him that he could sell and get a new home that was much more affordable, right-sized for him, and give him approximately $900,000 in the bank! The home mortgage loan he had taken out had been called because he couldn't pay it. He had been *borrowing* money to pay the loan. He started crying when I asked if I could call his daughter to explain the situation to her. He blew up at me and asked me to leave. He called me names and said I only cared about money. He didn't want to hear that if he didn't do something he would lose his home. I left feeling very sorry for him.

The Power of Rightsizing

There was also a couple in a beautiful retirement community. She had a powerful corporate job in New York. He had been self employed and done pretty well. They had a nice retirement nest egg and she had a nice corporate pension every month. They had social security as well. They moved to Texas and paid cash for a very nice golf course retirement home. They traveled and saw the world. She suddenly died of a heart attack. Now it seemed they were in a great position, but they never took into account *her* passing away. That rarely happens, women tend to outlive men. Gone ... not only was she gone, but he did not have rights of survivorship, so her pension and her social security were gone as well. They had about the same in social security. He went from a $10,000 per month income, $6,000 from her pension and $2,000 from her social security, to a $2,000 per month income. Not good. He was in quite a bind and it was apparent that he was running through his retirement nest egg like a hot knife through butter. He had a recommendation to meet with me from a friend who knew about his financial situation. He was not only taking a lot of money out of his retirement but paying taxes on the distributions as well–a double whammy. He had life insurance but she did not, and *he did not have rights of survivorship with her pension.* I put down my pen and stopped filling out a budget form and looked him straight in the eye. "You cannot continue to live this way," I told him.

He needed a plan: sell this very expensive home with very expensive overhead and country club membership, and downsize. The idea was to cut his expenses and *replace* his investment cash. I showed him how he could sell the home, purchase a smaller home or townhome using a reverse mortgage for purchase, and replace much of his investment retirement funds. I was busy doing the math and explaining how this could work and how he could *increase* his investment income instead of decreasing his investments. I mapped out a great plan. He started to cry and clenched his fists. "But this was our *DREAM* home and I cannot give it up." It was all too easy to show him how many months he had left in his investment accounts, and tell him how soon he would use up all his funds. He just got up and thanked me and left the room crying. I never felt so sorry for anyone. Unfortunately, the realtor friend who had referred him to me told me when the market crashed he had to sell the home to pay off all his debts and move into an apartment. Would have, could have, should have, but didn't–and he lost a lot when he didn't need to.

Moving can be a very painful, emotional change for some, and a real joy for others. What I keep saying is: have a plan. PLAN for changes–life continually changes for all of us. Some changes are predictable. Keep planning, keep the plan up to date, and follow the plan.

Here are two scenarios showing the power of reverse mortgage financing, enabling buyers to purchase a right-sized home later in life with no monthly payment. It is also a way to invest for retirement and have a new home that **pays them monthly.**

Couple–ages 78 and 80:

Sell Home and net:	$350,000		
Pay off Mortgage:	$120,000	Payment was:	$675.00 Monthly
Cash remaining:	$230,000		
Purchase New:	$250,000		
Cash to close:	$107,630		
Cash to invest:	$142,370	Interest 4%:	$473.00 Monthly Income
Monthly Payment–reverse mortgage:			$ 0
Monthly Budget Improved:			**$1,148.**

(Purchasers could not have bought home without financing or depleting retirement assets.)

Couple–ages 74 and 70:

Sell home and net:	$450,000		
Mortgage:	$0	Payment was:	$0 Monthly
Cash remaining:	$450,000		
Purchase New:	$450,000		
Cash to close:	$210,061		
Cash to invest:	$239,939	Interest 4%:	$799 Monthly Income
Monthly Payment– reverse mortgage:			$0
Monthly Budget Improved:			**$799**

(Purchasers now have retirement assets producing income and a new "Lifestyle" home with warranty.)

Fraud and Risk

*Beware of false prophets,
who come to you in sheep's clothing,
but inwardly they are ravenous wolves.*
Matthew 7:15

Who are the number one targets of fraud? Without a doubt–seniors. I have met with many victims who got severely financially hurt. My job has put me on the front lines of trying to repair the damage resulting from fraud. Working with banks definitely put me on the front lines because many victims go to their community banker first to get help. I hope some of these stories will serve as cautionary tales and help someone NOT be a victim.

I loved Bank of Oklahoma and spent much of my time going to sales meetings and teaching about reverse mortgage lending. One morning after I had earned my CSA designation, I was called to a bank in the mid-cities area. The manager was a great guy and a body builder–a huge guy. He ushered me into his office, warned me about the customer I was about to meet, then ran to the back of the bank. All I could think of was "Oh my, who am I going to meet?" In came this elderly couple, and the old gentleman was walking with a cane. Looked like he had had a hip replacement that hadn't gone well. His wife was really nice but very quiet. As I started to explain the program the old gentleman turned into a raging bear, screaming at me and swinging his cane. I thought I was going to get a really good whacking. The wife just sat there quietly. I was quiet, too. Finally I had had enough and was ready to show him the door. Then I remembered–I am a Certified Senior Advisor–I know what to do. Fortunately, he slowed his rage at me and I was able to get a word in. Instead of defending the program, or myself, I asked a simple question, "What happened?" Oh goodness, he dropped his head and quietly confessed that he had gotten into a bad investment program. Not only was it a fraud, but he had also taken out credit cards and charged $82,000 of credit card debt to finance his "great" investment. Needless to say he lost his $82,000 and was left holding that much in credit card debt. When his wife saw the bills and they started getting phone calls, all hell broke loose. If I was a betting man, the old gentlemen's rage was nothing compared to momma's rage when she

Fraud and Risk

found out. I ran the numbers and explained that this was a government-insured and regulated loan. He understood FHA and that we were an FDIC-regulated bank. He had been venting his anger–not only about what had happened to him, but to let me know if this was a scam he would beat the tar out of me. (In 2007 the sky had not fallen yet on the mortgage market, or I probably could never have convinced him this was a safe way to go.)

Instead of closing at a title company, I invited the couple back to the bank. I wanted to make sure we were in a safe environment in case the old man did a repeat performance. The manager showed me into the conference room and went and hid again. As I had done so many times before, I went through every document and carefully explained each one. I didn't want any mistakes and the title company closer wasn't very familiar with reverse mortgage documents. It took nearly two hours, but we got it closed. There was enough money to pay off all the credit card debt and have a little left over. They were really happy. No more debt or nasty phone calls, and no house payment! As we started to leave, the wife handed me a package that I opened. It was the most beautiful banana crème pie you have ever seen, decorated to the max. I hugged her under his watchful eye and shook his hand. He actually hugged me and had a tear in his eye. Man, I had done it, and no whipping with the cane! I gave the bank employees the pie and headed home. One of my friends commented when I told the story that "I bet that lady had to bake a mile of pies to make up for the husband's cane." I didn't care–I had won the day and the hearts of the bankers. From then on I got more calls. It's nice to be a hero.

The next instance of fraud came with a call from a small town outside of Oklahoma City. The couple was frantic and worried about losing their home. I jumped in my car and drove to see them. Their story was interesting, to say the least. They had lost $115,000 in a very well devised scam. A new "friend" they had met at church worked for this "specialty investment group" out of Florida. He had convinced them to invest $5,000 in a quick turn-around deal; they did, and within a month had their $5,000 back plus a huge profit. Thirty days and they had made money. So when he offered them the chance for a really big, sure-fire deal, they took out a home equity mortgage for $115,000 and gave it to him. About a month later he disappeared along with their $115,000. They went to local law enforcement and the district attorney and found that they weren't the only ones who had complained. Even their preacher had "invested" and everybody was looking for the guy. Charges were filed and they figured out that everything was false and a scam. As a result, they woke up to the fact that they had a big mortgage on their property and couldn't make the payments. They were in a panic to say the least. Unfortunately, the bank had a loan and it had to be paid. I was able to put together a reverse mortgage that eliminated the bank loan and eliminated their payment. They were thrilled. At the closing–I was handed a bag of cookies. Hey, I am making a living helping people and getting all kinds of goodies!

I tell this story to make the point–a con artist won their confidence, tricked them into a huge payment in only a couple of months. That deal and the loan on their home would have broken them. There was no way on their limited social security they could make the payments and survive. They took a giant risk they could *not* afford. Want to know what the investment was? He told them they were investing in big RV's for rock stars to use while on tour. Then the vehicles would be sold at a huge profit because they had become collector items because of the "rock stars" that had used them.

Why did they get taken? They were tired of living on meager social security income and just getting by. They wanted to earn some really big money and enjoy life. Unfortunately, it doesn't work that way. That kind of money requires long-term planning.

I had one man call me with a wonderful home worth over $750,000. He had retirement assets and was a retired attorney. He could have gotten nearly $400,000 out of his home, which was great. I was thinking he would surely be thrilled. Then I asked what he was going to do with the money. He wanted to buy gold futures, which is highly speculative. Gold had risen to an all-time high. Buying futures is different from buying gold. You are betting on a rising market, and if it doesn't rise you can lose and never own any gold. I took a deep breath and asked him if that wasn't a very risky venture to put his home equity into. I knew I was talking to someone I tremendously respected and who was very well educated, but I was talking to him like he was a teenager. He stopped for a minute and said, "Well, I know what I am doing." His wife who was sitting there finally spoke up and said she didn't like his idea. He was not a happy guy, so I left. I looked up the price of gold when I got home and wrote it down. A few months later the price of gold had dropped like a rock and lost a lot of its value. Oh what a world we live in. He would have lost all of the $400,000 and maybe more. Why was he willing to take such a risk? He wanted more income, more money, more cushion. High-risk opportunities are *not* the place for we seniors to invest unless we can easily afford to lose *all* the money.

I have also seen many sad situations that were not driven by a lack of money, but just the opposite. I have had two instances where widows in small towns received insurance money from their deceased husbands. Both of them had enough retirement income to be just fine. They had $100,000 plus cash bonuses and homes free and clear. They had no worries ... except they were lonely. So they started going out with friends, and it seemed everyone wanted to go to the local casino and party. If you are lonely and want to have a good time, why not? Long story made short, both ladies lost not only their insurance money, but leveraged their homes to the hilt and lost that money as well. One did a reverse mortgage so she was ok, just a little ashamed. The other spent what she had taken out and now she was about to lose her home. I spent hours on the phone with her until I got the whole story after talking to her daughter: Mom was about to lose her home and she was short $15,000 to do a reverse mortgage. I couldn't believe it–Mom had dropped over $250,000 in an Oklahoma casino, which included all the home equity loan proceeds from her formerly paid-off home. She cried and cried, and all she could say was "I was just so lonely." Her daughter, who had also given her a lot of money, was by now furious. Needless to say, casinos are not in the business to lose money. Gambling is *NOT* investing – it's a bad deal, especially when you cannot afford to lose.

Unfortunately, unknown criminals don't always perpetrate the biggest forms of senior fraud–many times it's family members. The drunken son who cannot keep a job and lives with Mom, takes her credit cards, and uses the ATM machine like it's *his* bank account, not Mom's. I have sat across tables with destitute widows who cannot understand why they are overdrawn. Guess what Mom? Your son, the addict, stole your money for drugs and booze. I have even confronted these guys, and in each case I was told where to go in no uncertain terms. It is as if they demand the right to take the money from their own mothers. It's not gender specific, either. I have heard stories of daughters doing the same thing. It's sad. The parent, for whatever reason, feels they have to support the messed-up child. They make every excuse for them and write another check. I stopped a loan from going through when I found out that Grannie was doing the loan in order for her grandson to have a new corvette. One quick call to Dad (Grannie's son) put a stop to that.

Several tragic cases of fraud were a result of caretakers stealing all the money and everything in sight. I met with the lady who had become a court-appointed guardian and found that the 98 year old's substantial retirement funds, over $500,000, had been slowly skimmed off by her former caretaker. The way they found out was the caretaker had a stroke and died. The 98 year old had no family and, as a result, friends stepped in and helped her get a guardian. The guardian called me and found all the money was gone, all the jewelry was gone, and most of the art was gone. All that was left was her home. She was a wonderful, gracious lady who had been a New York Radio City Music Hall Rockette as a young lady, and had toured with the USO during WWII. She never had children, but her husband had left her well off and in the hands of a "trusted" caretaker. Had the caretaker not died, goodness only knows what else would have been stolen. But now, all the money was gone. The guardian and I developed a budget and a program using a reverse mortgage to supplement her income so the lady could stay in her home.

Another lady in Norman, Oklahoma, suffered a major stroke. Her husband had been a retired Army Colonel and she had about $5,000 a month income from his retirement and social security. She had several caretakers who took shifts twenty-four hours a day to take care of her. Her mind was sharp as a tack, but her body was paralyzed as a result of the stroke. I recommended *against* the reverse mortgage and suggested she get help from her doctor to find a full care facility that could provide supervised medical help. You would have thought I had said something horrible–she blew a gasket. I called both of her sons and talked to her grandson. I explained that, in my opinion, she needed to be where she could have competent medical care and not off-the-street minimum-wage baby sitters. All of them said the same thing, "You know how *Momma* is." Yes, I said, meaner than a junkyard dog with a temper like a tornado. So I did the loan and we put $163,000 in her bank account. About a year later one of her sons called–I recognized the caller ID. My first question was, how was Momma? It wasn't good. He had visited her to find the caretakers had stolen almost all of her money, sold her medicines, and left her in a mess. He found an awful situation and immediately moved her into a nursing home. She lasted only about three weeks and was gone. The year of no medicine and no real medical care had taken its toll. The house was a mess and almost everything of value gone. Credit cards were maxed out and defaulted, and guess where the caretakers were? Nowhere to be found. Her stubbornness and mean streak had been rewarded with theft and a sad death.

Fraud against seniors is rampant. Some think it's because they are feeble, or have lost their ability to reason. This is sometimes true, but many times even those negative situations could have been improved by having a plan and getting the right help. Also, standing up to family members who abuse them requires help from inside the family, and sometimes a neutral third party from outside the family. Willingness to focus on a plan and paying attention helps everyone. It is easy for the senior to get emotional, "I am so lonely," or wanting to be needed, which can lead to enabling. I tell seniors to get involved in a church. Find trustworthy advisors who can help them. Volunteer in positive groups. Reimagine life and find new fulfillment. Stay away from people who gamble and party too much. Find friends who share a common interest(s). One of the reasons so many seniors get taken advantage of is they tend to isolate. They are ashamed to let people know what is really going on. Isolation may be a way to hide problems, but it is also a sure-fire way to have a scam artist take advantage of you. Isolation is not a good thing, especially for seniors.

Attitude Determines Altitude

*A merry heart does good, like medicine,
but a broken spirit dries the bones.*
Proverbs 17:22

Throughout these stories there is always a lesson to be learned about money and the use of money. My generation, the Baby Boomer generation, has more mixed up views about money than just about any other. Our parents were children during the great depression and our grandparents suffered, struggled, and paid a hefty price. Their attitudes had a huge impact on us and an even bigger impact on them. I have been fortunate to meet some people with really great attitudes and now I can tell their stories.

As a Certified Senior Advisor, my customers for the first part of my career were born between 1920 and 1940. That definitely meant they were children during the great depression. Therefore many of them have a great deal of fear when it comes to money. They remember when families lost their homes and farms to the banks. There were call provisions in almost every mortgage and, even if you were current and paying your mortgage, the bank or whoever took over the bank could call the note and foreclose on your home. When the banks failed, many suffered. As a result, people didn't trust banks or debt. We also lived in an agricultural economy. One disaster led to another and fear became a driving force. Fear led a lot of people to make decisions that have not always been good; or make no decision at all, which can be worse.

Because of all that happened during the depression, our parents worked hard and paid their homes off. They believed that until the mortgage was paid off you didn't own your home, the bank did. In the meantime, laws were passed to protect homeowners–homestead laws and other laws regarding banking. The driving force behind having the home paid off still tends to be the underlying fear of losing your home to the bank, even though the laws have been changed to safeguard the homeowner.

Other attitudes also prevailed. I remember too many men who suffered long and hard in jobs they hated because of fear of not having a paycheck. Too many of them had heart attacks and lived miserably. Fear guided many of their decisions. I have a close friend whose dad died in his 50's. I remember his dad and his childhood and how World War II shaped him. He was a generally unhappy man who had a government job he hated, but one that meant security. He was typical of many – miserable and barely making ends meet.

Fear of lack of money was a plague that influenced this generation. While some took risks and many fortunes were made, the average family saved and saved and saved. What I have seen time and time again is they are now paralyzed and cannot make decisions–which leads to negative consequences. Also, this generation is the longest-lived generation ever. The average life span has increased by over thirty years. Also, as a generation, we have seen the greatest technological changes in the history of the world. Yet all too often this generation is lost when it comes to technology. They are also frequently lost when it comes to money. Call it old age or fear or whatever–they have become easy prey for fraud and can be the most disconnected generation ever. Nothing is the same for them as it once was–church, cars, communication–the whole world has changed so much. No longer do families live together, protecting each other. In many cases, I have seen pride cause seniors to go without. Isolation, fear, and lack become a big part of many seniors' lives. Change is fraught with fear for them because the changes we are seeing in our culture are so tremendous that they feel left behind. Have you ever been on a freeway and passed an elderly person or couple doing 55 miles per hour while traffic is doing 75 or 80? They are terrified – too much of their life is like that.

How do we help them? Encouragement, interaction, involvement, and understanding are keys to helping anyone. Pay attention to seniors and interact. Be understanding and caring. I see impatience in families and other frustrations. Lots of family stresses and strains come out when Mom and Dad become really old. What is important is protecting family members and making sure smart decisions are made using all their assets to their benefit. Sometimes they might not like it, but "right-sizing" can be the best thing for them to improve their cash flow and quality of life.

Then there is my generation ... sex, drugs, and rock and roll ... definitely some different views about money. The Baby Boomer generation has had more influence on the financial markets and our culture than any other in history. I was a 1965 graduate from high school and I know, I lived through all of it. By and large, my generation didn't save for retirement. It is estimated by surveys that between 95 to 97% of the Baby Boomer generation has no savings, no plan, and no assets other than Social Security. This is not good for our country. All politics aside, over 3,650,000 people per year turn 65 and about 3,500,000 do not have anything other than government programs to rely on–and maybe their home. Really scary – many of that group every year are moving from full employment to social security income. Many pensions have failed or been done away with, and in most states teacher retirement or other retirement programs are about the same as Social Security. Did you know the average Social Security monthly payment in America is $1,385.00 per person? So someone earning maybe $4,000 to $5,000 per month drops down to less than $1,500 on average. That is a huge drop in buying power and it compounds year after year. After working with economic development I know that number has a multiplier effect of about four–so instead of impacting 3,500,000 people per year, you are really affecting nearly 14,000,000 people PER YEAR. That is scary, because a lot of Baby Boomers unpreparedness will impact everyone. So what can be done?

First of all, many of us will have to keep on working, me included. We will have to find new careers and new opportunities. Retirement isn't just postponed, it is redefined–a new way of life. Baby Boomers need to wake up and take a look at their assets. If they have a mortgage, can they "right-size" and end up with no debt to improve cash flow and use some of those funds to invest in retirement? Can long-term health care be bought? Can money be put away? Is it wise to upgrade to that lake house dream home, or focus on cash flow? Focusing on cash flow is about the most difficult thing for people to do. What do all the commercials say? "You deserve this new ..." Well, maybe you deserve to pay YOURSELF first by putting savings away, NOW. Dave Ramsey is a financial teacher who focuses on paying off credit cards and building wealth for those still in their earning years. His Financial Peace lessons are great. Unfortunately, not everyone heard his instruction in time. We as a generation need to change and focus on cash flow now and saving as much as we can before it's too late.

I want to make one other point. Fear of money is a driving force. The Bible says ... the love of money is a root of all *kinds of* evil ... (1Tim 6:10) Money can be a tool for accomplishment or a curse. 85% of all the lottery winners are bankrupt in 5 years. That means they spent and borrowed more than they received. We live like drunken sailors and take on debt like there's no tomorrow. Take a look at the national debt. The politicians have done it, too. Debt is so easy to get into, and so hard to get out of. So when we invest, we need to be prudent. Get-rich-quick schemes are usually scams. Good returns are hard to find, just like good jobs. Investing in the stock market (or anything) is risky and requires lots of homework, knowledge, and prudence.

I have a degree in finance from the University of Texas at Austin. One of my last class assignments was to analyze a company as if I were investing. I drew a new high tech company in San Diego. I looked up everything I could find about them and it all sounded great. Then I knew the company my Dad worked for had a major development in San Diego, so I called him. When I asked about this company, he started laughing. How did you get that one, he asked? Well it turned out my Dad's company was actually my assigned company's landlord. Then I found out they were behind on their rent, and their "high tech" solutions were electronic lobster pots. What!?!? I asked? So this deal was an over-promoted, unrealistic gamble – definitely a bad deal. My analysis included the "Landlord's" report that they were behind on rent, and got me an A+. The lesson I learned was to dig deep and ask questions. Do not take anything at face value. If it sounds too good to be true, it probably is.

So how do people fall for fraudulent deals? When they hear about "great deals" it gives them hope that they can make up for hard times. Yes there are deals and will be deals like Apple and Microsoft. But for every one of those huge skyrocketing deals there have been plenty of deals like the San Diego company–all hype.

I counseled a man in Ardmore, Oklahoma who came to me devastated. He had inherited a home and $350,000 from his father. He had worked hard all his life but hadn't done very well. His social security was limited and he wanted to be wise. He went to a stockbroker and invested the $350,000, but he wanted high returns. He wanted a life in retirement he had never known. The stockbroker put him in Bernie Madoff's investment deal. All of his money was lost. Madoff went to jail and hundreds of millions of dollars were lost to his Ponzi scheme. Why? Investors thought they could get 15% returns when the market was paying at best 5%. It was an illegal scheme to steal people's money.

If you saw the movie The Big Short you saw how so many were scammed and how our whole country was hurt in the mortgage mess of 2008. There were a few, a very few investment groups who did the research and knew the truth. I remember one scene in the movie when they went to Florida to look at some of the homes in the bond portfolios and found some empty and many were complete messes. The ones who did their research made a killing shorting the mortgage market. Too many lost too much.

What lessons do Baby Boomers need to learn? Good money management starts with saving and investing wisely after much research. We must also *stay* active and reinvent ourselves. Most of us need to keep working and producing, not just for financial wellbeing, but also mental acuity. Staying active, informed, and involved leads to a joyful, interesting life. Sitting on the couch is a sad way to die. *Not* paying attention leads to real disaster.

Reimagine Reinvent Renew

*Be strong and of good courage;
do not be afraid, nor be dismayed,
for the Lord your God is with you wherever you go.
Joshua 1:9b*

Life is all about change and as we grow older it seems like the changes can become overwhelming. I have met some wonderful people who changed their lives in great and positive ways. They have been an inspiration to me and hopefully they will inspire you as well.

One of the neatest stories is about a wonderful lady in Oklahoma City. Her husband had been a carpenter and they had a modest but very nice home. He died of a massive heart attack and left no life insurance. He had been self-employed all his life and had put very little into social security and none into retirement. The net result was she had a $675.00 monthly payment from social security, which was the same as her mortgage payment.

She had been living on baby sitting, donations, and was literally destitute. When we sat down in her home she handed me a plate of the best lemon drop cookies I had ever had. She loved to bake and she loved her church. She was a wonderful lady and she told me she trusted in the LORD and trusted her banker and as a result, trusted me. When the appraisal came in, it was lower than expected. To me it felt like a racial issue because she was African American in a predominantly white part of town. We were short of the funds she needed and the reverse mortgage just wouldn't cover the payoff of the mortgage. The call I made to her really made me feel bad. She said, "Jimmy, I trust in the LORD and I trust you, and I'll be praying for the right outcome." Each week for about a month I made that call, and in the meantime I also called every realtor I knew to try to find comparable sales that could change the appraisal and fix the mess.

Each week she said the same words of faith. I felt terrible because she needed it so badly and she was such a wonderful lady. She had no family to help her, either. Then one day I read a fax that FHA had changed the reverse mortgage program and raised the loan amounts. I quickly reran the numbers and there we were. We could not only pay off her mortgage but give her about $4,000 as well. I was jumping for joy. That was a fun phone call. We got the loan done. I drove to her home for the closing and another lemon drop cookie. That was a great day. I asked her, Mrs. B, what are you planning to do now that you have no mortgage payment and some cash? She told me she had already signed up at a local junior college for courses in medical billing, and two doctors in her church wanted her to do their billing. She was ready to buy a computer and get started. Last time I talked to her she was not only doing fine, but making a very good living and putting money away. She had reinvented herself as a businesswoman. She also told me she was baking cookies for the church socials more often, and I'll bet you could find some of her cookies in doctor's offices, as well.

Using all your assets wisely and having a plan is so important. I met a lady who had been a corporate executive and decided to take early retirement. She had a wonderful retirement account but she wanted to wait to take her social security. She did have a very nice home and a mortgage payment. She told me she wanted to do more, but needed to either sell her home or do a reverse mortgage to end the monthly payments. I met with her and her son, and we were able to pay off the mortgage, with a little left over. She told me her life dream had been to take care of children and teach. She had a plan to go back to school and get her teaching certificate and work with children. She soon took a job teaching kindergarten. The money she made covered her living expenses plus a summer cruise for a vacation. She was able to defer taking any distributions from her retirement and from social security and maximized both over time. She had a budget and a plan and she looked forward to working as long as she could. My guess is she now has a huge retirement and a very happy life. That was reimagining her life–she did it.

I have many stories of people who wanted to change their lives, but financially didn't feel they could afford to take the risk. One man I met was a great project manager for an apartment building company. He had lost his job of 30 years with the same company in Dallas and, at his age, over 65, no one wanted him. He had a three-acre, beautiful fenced ranchette and nice home. He was a cowboy at heart. His wife had died and now he only had one social security income instead of two, and a mortgage on the home. We got the mortgage paid off. That made his life a lot better and enabled him to keep his home. I told him the story about the corporate lady who was now a teacher. That sparked an idea, and he went to the local high school and found out they wanted to have construction as a trade to teach high-school kids. He was their man, and he started that fall teaching construction from the ground up. I heard that someone donated a lot and another donated building materials to the program. He had those kids actually build a home! He told me his plan to sell that house and buy another lot and the materials to plow back into the program so that his next year's students would have the same experience of building a home. He was teaching what he had learned all his life and loving it. He was renewing and teaching AND making a living. I heard several years later from his daughter that he had a heart attack and had passed away suddenly. I know he left a legacy of kids who learned construction in a powerful way and could make a good living, thanks to him. In the meantime he enjoyed his years to the full.

I have seen numerous "new" authors write books. One gentleman in my church has penned a series of travel adventures. He worked all over the world in his career so, when he writes a story about an adventure in some far away place, it has authenticity. He has been there. Another man was furious about events he saw unfolding regarding Vietnam veterans. He wrote a book titled Stolen Valor. I had lunch with him and was fascinated by his stories of what really happened in Vietnam and how the press distorted news to create headlines. People claimed to be heroes when they never served or were never near Vietnam. Read his book "Stolen Valor"–you are not only reading about a tragic time in our nation's history, but you are reading an author who reinvented himself.

From becoming teachers, to authors, to inventors, to following a life-long passion, I see people reimagining their lives and living anew all the time. Just because we turn 65 or 70 doesn't mean we are old, unless we let ourselves act that way. Age is real, but I ask the question all the time "Are you living to die, or dying to live?" Are you really enjoying life by accomplishing what you were never able to do before? How many stories do we hear about seniors graduating from college later in life? I met an electrical engineer in Houston who was Hispanic. His passion was to teach seniors and kids how to use computers. Guess what, teenagers? The 60's generation *INVENTED* computers! What he did was great. I helped him not have a mortgage payment, and he was able to travel and put on workshops to develop computer skills.

A wonderful schoolteacher in Oklahoma City was sent to me by her niece. She had had a stroke and was in a wheel chair with her left hand tucked under her chest. We developed a plan to do improvements to her home. A wheel chair ramp and handicapped bathrooms were needed, as well as some minor repairs. The niece's husband organized a few friends and they got it done. We also replaced the windows in the garage with Lexan so kids who liked to throw rocks couldn't break them. They did a lot of painting and repairing. While getting the reverse mortgage through processing, I had a heart attack. I called the niece and told her I had been in the hospital for three days and her aunt's deal was delayed.

She asked how I was and I told her the weekend before I had walked 5 miles in Ruidoso, New Mexico (at 7,500 feet altitude) and three days after having a stent put in I had walked three miles – no heart damage. When I had my first meeting with her aunt, I asked if she could walk–she could with great difficulty. However, her aunt was not about to be outdone by this fat ol' Texan, so she got a walker and, although struggling to walk, made it to the end of the block and back. Six months later she was walking a mile and a half a day and had lost sixty pounds. As a result she was able to get off some of her medicine, like diabetes, and was able to drive her car again. She recovered from her stroke and started tutoring kids again in her home. Now THAT is renewal, physically and mentally. Good thing I was from Texas–that motivated her to get up out of that wheel chair and show me up. Best response I have ever seen.

Planning to Change

*A prudent man foresees evil and hides himself,
but the simple pass on and are punished.*
Proverbs 22:3

Several years ago I volunteered in a halfway house for teenage boys coming out of the Texas juvenile justice system, more commonly known as reform school. It seemed they had no chance in life. They had been brought up in mostly fatherless homes with no idea how to achieve success. Most of them seemed destined to return to the streets and to adult prison. So I wrote a book and started teaching it to them. "Planning to Change" is all about planning for the future for young men at a major turning point in life. Guess what? I see the same kind of turning point happening in the senior community. 95% of seniors have no plan for retirement other than social security. Many are terribly unhappy in dead-end jobs, and when the day comes to walk out the door, they go home to a lazy boy. Oh, they may play golf for a while or travel, but somewhere inside they seem to quit. I submit that all people need purpose in life and achievement. We need to feel like we are accomplishing something and earning our way. Not everyone is that way, but let me startle you. From the statistics I have seen, I believe that 95% of the seniors are totally unprepared for their future. 10,000 people a day are turning 65–us Baby Boomers. Do the math–a staggering number of people are moving into retirement with nothing more than social security and a home. Few have actually paid off their home by the time they retire.

The economic burden of that is unthinkable. Let me give you a few other statistics. Only 3% of the American population has long-term health care insurance other than Medicare or Medicaid. That means 97% of us are expecting a government bailout ... not very likely. Every financial advisor or stockbroker I have talked to lately recognizes that only about 5% of the population has retirement assets. Less than 40% of Americans have a will. When I ask about durable powers of attorney, eyes glaze over and people ask, "What's that?" What am I telling you? As a group, we have no plan. Without a plan we are doomed to fail – a very painful prospect – not just for us, but for the whole country.

Planning to Change

Let's *face* the reality of change and CHANGE financially, physically, medically, mentally, and every other way we need to. One of the best plans I have seen came when I was called to Granbury to meet with a family. The husband was so proud because he had survived so many heart attacks and open-heart surgery. He opened his shirt to show me more scars than I had ever seen. They had spent all of their retirement money on hospitals and doctor bills. They had bought this wonderful lake house with cash and were set until he started down heart attack alley. He wanted to make a plan. He knew that he couldn't get life insurance and when he passed she would lose the lesser of their two social securities. They were managing quite well on nearly $4,000 per month, but he knew if he went she would only have about $2,000 per month to live on. So we discussed options and built a plan.

They did the reverse mortgage and didn't take any funds but had a line of credit. The line has a decent growth rate–the longer it goes the more it grows. When he or she passes, the other has the line to draw on. We planned out five years and it all worked. The line of credit with the growth rate would grow to replace what they had lost to medical bills. She could stay in the home if she wanted to or sell and use the equity to relocate. If she didn't use the line, it would keep growing. If she didn't use it *she didn't have to pay it back*–that kept the maximum amount of equity in her home. Now they had a plan and it worked for them. They had peace of mind and access to money if it was needed. The good news– he is still with us and they are enjoying life. He also eats right and exercises daily. That guy is loving life ... dying to *live*, not living to die.

I have had many couples sit down with me over the years that were not old enough for a reverse mortgage, but wanted to have a plan. I start with a budget and show how to get out of debt except for their home. I also show how much they will be able to get with a reverse mortgage when they reach retirement age. When we get through they have a goal, a budget for now, and a budget for when they retire. I also suggest getting legal estate planning help–wills, powers of attorney, medical directives, and the legal planning for the day when bad things happen to good people. With a plan and assets, surviving a storm is a lot easier.

Now, about legal planning: One guy called me whose wife had recently died. He was experiencing that loss of her social security income. He wanted to do a reverse mortgage to supplement the income. Only problem was she didn't have a will. I asked if she had a previous marriage and any children. Yes–she had two boys and they had a child. He hung up on me when I told him that,

Planning to Change

without a will, those two boys were half owners of his home. About two hours later he called me back and he was very nice. He had talked to an attorney and I was right. The attorney was going to charge him "thousand$" to correct his problem. I suggested we could have the title company do affidavits of heirship and deeds, the boys could sign them, and we could then vest title in him. He was taken care of at a fraction of the cost. Title companies do that all the time for customers. He got real quiet and when he spoke I could hear the shakiness in his voice. "So what is the problem?" I asked. He confided in me that both boys were in Huntsville state prison. Oops–that *was* a problem. In about two days he called me and, because he had been such a good husband and taken care of their mom during her cancer, the boys agreed. We went forward. He drove to Huntsville with all the documents and someone notarized them at the prison for him. It could have been a very different story. He was very fortunate.

I do a radio show in Dallas for veterans and first responders–Alliance 4 the Brave. I asked an estate-planning attorney on my show to talk about the need for proper legal planning. He told me a story that was an eye opener. A young woman who was 28 was killed with her 6-year-old daughter in a car wreck by an 18-wheeler on Interstate 45 near Conroe. The young woman also had a

2-year-old little girl who was staying with a baby sitter. She had no will, no planning for what should happen with the children. She also had no husband and no family to be found. The two year old became a ward of the state. In addition, a wrongful death suit was filed and the court awarded the baby $7,500,000 from the trucking company. What Clarke then told me was tough to hear. Several men showed up claiming to be the baby's father – what a mess. I asked what happened and all he said was she was still a ward of the state. Robin, our program's founder, heard the show and met with the law firm *the next week* and had all her estate planning documents done. It got her attention and she took care of things.

Wills can be critically important. I don't know how many horrible financial and family messes I have seen as a result of no will or a will written on a sheet of yellow paper. That may work in the movies, but real life requires real legal help. What you spend now will save everyone a fortune and heartache later.

Sometimes I shudder at *why* people don't plan for the future. I have had people tell me that they have a will, done 30 years ago, but they just cannot remember where they put it. I recommend a legal check up every 5 years because laws change … *everything* changes.

Trusts can be a needed legal vehicle to take care of estate issues when they are properly done. They should

Planning to Change

include everything. I don't know how many times I have sat with someone in tears whose stepparent took everything out of spite and threw away treasured keepsakes. I tell people if it's a family heirloom, give it to the family member *now*–don't wait.

Durable powers of attorney are critical legal documents. I know there is a popular TV show "The Living Dead." I have seen it happen and it is tragic. A beloved senior has a stroke or dementia or Alzheimer's and there is no legal way to take over other than a court-appointed guardianship. Trust me on this–you don't want a court-appointed *anything*. Things take forever to get done, they are expensive, and they are almost impossible to deal with.

I was asked by a realtor to meet with her some time ago. I had met her mother some years before and I knew of her, but didn't really know her. The mom had been in a terrible auto accident with an uninsured driver–an illegal. She had severe brain trauma, so the daughter had an attorney draw up a power of attorney, but it was too late. No doctor would attest that she was competent to sign it, because she wasn't. Legally the daughter had no say. The banks went ahead and handled everything, but when it came to trying to do a reverse mortgage or any loan, she was blocked. In fact, most title companies will not transfer title using a power of attorney without verification that the person who signed the document was capable of signing it. To make matters worse, Mom had a stroke and went from bad to worse. I don't know what happened or how they ended up, but from where I sat they were in a pickle. I also have a friend with a wife who has Alzheimer's, and he wants to do things with his business and home. He has been waiting over two months for the court judge to approve what he needs to do. Every time he has to call the attorney it costs money–OUCH.

I knew a couple that were terribly injured in a traffic accident. A large SUV ran a red light and hit their car late one night after a church party. They survived, but he was little more than a vegetable, and she was in very bad shape physically and mentally. That truck was doing 65 MPH when it hit them and it was a mess. There was no family on either side and no children. They both became wards of the state. No will, no directives–nothing to direct anyone how to take care of either of them.

I also wish I could tell you how many times in small towns someone has bought a home and paid cash, never thinking to get a **title insurance policy**. They just went to some attorney's office and paid their money and got a deed. Part of title insurance is getting a clear title. We had one that we worked on for four months trying to clear title. Two sisters had inherited a home from their parents and one sister died in 1973. When the other sister died her son sold the home to a lady without a title policy. She

Planning to Change

married, and when she died her will passed the home on to her husband. He wanted to do a reverse mortgage, but the title company could not give clear title. Remember the sister who died in 1973? There was *no recorded will or probate*. When the house was sold there was the possibility of not having a clear title. We found out that there were 77 heirs possibly entitled to the property. My client, a nice elderly gentleman, was totally confused. With this title issue he could not finance or sell the home, and there was a remote chance someone could come along and sue as a possible heir. This is a title company nightmare. His friend helped the man and 77 letters were sent out. Fortunately, one of the possible heirs was the wife of the attorney who had sold the house to my client's wife. They found a will dated in the 1960's when the women inherited the home, giving her 50% to her sister. We were able to clear title and get it done. Had the lady not remembered the will AND kept all of her husband's records, we could still be trying to close that loan. You say to yourself, "That's complicated!" and it was. Had that will been probated in 1973 there never would have been a problem. Had the lady used a title company when she bought the house in the 1980's it would have been solved then. If this had not been straightened out, the old gentleman, my client, would never be able to sell the home and provide clear title. See my point?

Using the resources you have, and planning ahead with proper documentation, can save a fortune in legal bills and your home.

Time and time again I warn people to prepare. What did I say? 95% of us are not prepared. That is a problem that we can solve. Managing change is about making a plan and following it.

Mental and Physical Challenges

... reaching forward to those things which are ahead ...
Phil 3:13c

I have been really fortunate to meet David Vobora who started the Adaptive Training Foundation (www.AdaptiveTrainingFoundation.org). He trains the broken men and women who have been severely injured in combat. Watch their videos and you will see amputees do amazing things. They have a will to live and a zest for life. Even broken and battered they exercise and help each other out. Ever see a man with no arms or legs working out and sweating in the gym? When we let challenges defeat us our quality of life can be destroyed and that affects everyone around us. This is an area so many need to change.

Have any idea how often I walk into a home and the borrower has the TV blaring, an ashtray full of cigarette butts, and a 32-ounce Big Gulp or beer by their chair?

Hello? Are we *trying* to kill ourselves? I know smoking can be one of the hardest habits to break, but if you have seen friends and family die of lung cancer as I have, you understand how ugly and deadly it is. It isn't worth it. It's also devastating for everyone around the smoker.

Now let's talk about mental exercise. Reading, talking, and being involved is huge. Studies have shown active people enjoy a better quality of life. Today my Dad is 96 years old. He reads and listens to books on tape. Do *not* get in a current events discussion with him–he reads the Dallas newspaper, the Wall Street Journal, and the Sunday New York Times. He uses a reading machine for his macular degeneration, but he gets it read. He also goes to his club and works out several times a week. He stays active and keeps his mind active–the quality of his life is excellent.

Once I was in San Francisco with a business partner, Joe, who took me to the famous Blue Fox restaurant. The waiter, very spry and full of energy, knew Joe and ordered for us. Great meal, great service. Near the end of the meal he asked Joe, who seemed in his 70's, if he wanted to go walking in the morning. Joe said absolutely and they agreed to meet at our hotel, the Hyatt Embarcadero. Joe asked me how old I thought his waiter friend was? I thought a minute and said probably about your age–in his 70's. The answer: 95! I was shocked.

Mental and Physical Challenges

Joe and his waiter friend walked at 6 AM the streets and hills of San Francisco for five miles. (I slept in and met them for coffee. ;-)

Many seniors I have met stay very active and connected. They exercise, read, use their minds, and enjoy life. And they are a joy to be around. I love my weekly lunches with my Dad and friends, and guess who *leads* a lively discussion? That's right – the 96 year old!

On the other hand I see people all the time who are physically and mentally in terrible shape. In many cases they don't make real good judgments, either. Remember the lady in Norman who was really tough and mean? I talked to someone who manages a nursing rehab facility and related that story. She told me of patients they had like my teacher friend who had strokes and had gone through rehab and recovered quite a bit of not only mobility but also health. It wasn't just the medicine and the rehab, but the *interaction* with others and the *stimulation*. The lady in Norman might still be alive today and in her home had she not been so defiant.

I was very fortunate because Joe, my former business partner, was an exercise and health nut. He belonged to Cooper Clinic–a huge exercise club in Dallas. Dr. Ken Cooper wrote the book on aerobic exercise and I got to know him, thanks to Joe. I also had a membership in the Aerobics Center. One day I noticed a tall very slender elderly gentleman who I seemed to see every time I was there. One day Joe introduced me to Karl. He was in his late 70's and walked five miles every morning and five miles every afternoon and sat in the hot tub. Wow, I said to myself that is dedication. I asked Dr. Cooper about it and he told me Karl had severe arthritis. If he didn't walk every day he would lock up and become crippled. Walking every day kept Karl going. He had a routine–after his walk he went to his office and worked all day as a financial advisor. Then he drove *back* to the Aerobics Center and walked *again*. One day I didn't see Karl–Dr. Cooper told me he had had a stroke. Joe and I went to see him at Presbyterian Hospital. When we entered the room Karl sat up and offered us a chair. He looked perfectly fine except for the hospital gown and IV. The stroke had hardly affected him. In a few days he was back on the track. That was a long time ago and as far as I know Karl continued on for many years. He is one of my heroes – a shining light that inspires me.

Working, keeping active physically and mentally, keeps us healthy. On the other hand, I had a high school friend who sold his business and went home. After two months of golf he came home and sat back in the Lazy Boy and quit everything. I don't know how it happened, but he lasted about two more months. That was not a fun funeral to attend for a guy in his mid 60's.

Mental and Physical Challenges

One day, I was sitting in a minister's office talking about his church. He had become a good friend and he had a church in Oak Cliff. As we shared coffee and stories I could hear a lawn mower going. "Did you see my yard man?" he asked me. "No, but it sounds like he is really moving along." The minister laughed and told me when I left to introduce myself to his 96 year old church member who insisted on mowing the lawn and taking care of the grounds. That was one really happy old guy taking care of his church. Praise the LORD for his example.

Finally, I am a good example. I used to walk a lot, three to four miles a day. As I mentioned I had walked 5 miles in Ruidoso New Mexico at 7,500 feet of altitude before my heart attack. I do like to cook and I am a husky, big-shouldered guy. Actually, overweight is the correct term – but not for long. My walking and exercise is what made my heart attack not be a bad one. I had no heart damage as a result. It has been three years now and I am exercising 5-6 days a week. Exercising by pushing away from the table would be even better! I am working on that.

My knee started hurting as a result of an injury from a horse years ago. Not much cartilage left in the left knee. My doctor suggested exercising it and showed me how. When I started it had become so bad I could hardly walk up a flight of stairs and I couldn't walk around the block without help. I was in pain. After two months of an hour each day on a recumbent bike, the exercise strengthened that knee without pounding it. I now run up a flight of stairs at the workout center and at home. And I can walk without pain. No surgery, no gimmicks, just regular supplements and an hour a day of exercise. Everyone tells me I look better, too. I have lost some weight. Maybe I can actually do a push up in a few more weeks. I feel better, my clothes fit better, and my stamina is improved. What more can I say?

Don't let the changes aging creates beat you. Do what you can and **find the fun**. Exercise is important, both mental and physical. Use it or lose it.

Stay Plugged In

*... not forsaking the assembling of ourselves together ...
but exhorting one another, and so much the more
as you see the Day approaching.*
Hebrews 10:25

What I see happening time and time again is isolation. An elderly person loses their spouse and they stop going out. They stop interacting with friends. In many cases the old friends are gone and they feel all alone. They become more and more isolated. The familiar home, the dependence on family to run their errands, and they don't want to get out. Fear of falling or having an accident immobilizes some. Their life becomes focused on fear. They watch TV, look at the headlines, and freeze. The church or community center they once loved is a distant memory. They just don't go out, except maybe to doctor appointments. They don't interact and as a result they become more and more fearful. They cannot conceive of relocating, either to a child's home or a retirement home or anywhere because what is familiar is right here – their home. Some of that is dementia and some of it is just fear-driven inertia. People frequently lose motivation. They start living just to die, instead of dying to live.

How you live your life determines your quality of life. I am certain of that. Watching daytime TV will rot anyone's brain–that is for sure. What can you do? Ask for help. Ask someone to take you to church. Offer to take your grandkids to McDonalds, even if they are 40. Go to senior centers and learn new things. My Dad and stepmom love to go hear lectures at SMU. Get involved with family, and with church. Meet new people and do new things. My wife's mom, Alli, took us to a cheese factory for a Saturday lesson on how to make mozzarella. Talk about fun! That was a great birthday for me. Go to movies with friends. Learn to use a computer so you can email your grand kids.

One lady I talked to was so sad and lamented that her grandkids never called or saw her. I asked if she had a cell phone–yes she did. Did she know how to text message? Kids don't call, they text. Email is how people communicate and schedule events. The Internet can be a wonderful resource, and there are lots of people who teach seniors how to use it and not let it abuse them. So she did. Now she texts her grandkids, and me, and sees everyone on a regular basis. Granny is hip and cool – oops, those were the terms of my day. Sorry.

Caretakers

... 'Assuredly, I say to you, inasmuch as you did it to one of the least of these My brethren, you did it to Me.'
Matthew 25:40

Some of the most challenging changes in anyone's life are having serious health problem(s) or having a loved one with serious health problem(s). I haven't even counted how many families came to me for a reverse mortgage to get funds to pay for caretaking. It's a serious problem that faces many and a problem we need to understand and face.

The hardest change is for the person who has become disabled. It is no fun to find ourselves in a dependent situation. I have seen too many of these changes and their consequences. Strokes, cancer, dementia, Alzheimer's, brain injury, amputation, loss of sight, you name the disability and I have seen it. It hurts beyond belief to become disabled, either mentally or physically. However, what

I have seen and experienced: **Attitude is 90 percent of the battle.** I have seen many veterans, including one who lost all four limbs, and I have seen every response imaginable. Whatever happened, it isn't the end of the world, but it may feel like it. I told you about the lady who had a stroke. To show me up, this (less and less) fat ol' Texan, she started walking. She went from a wheel chair, being very sad, and feeling defeated, to being a victor. She lost weight and got off a lot of medication. She is driving again. Attitude and exercise is the key.

As a result of my radio show I was introduced to a brain health clinic in Dallas. Cerebrum Health does amazing work with traumatic brain injury. They use state of the art diagnostics and equipment to retrain the brain. Yes, our brains can be retrained after injury. I asked for a story when I talked to them on the air, and they told me of a 15-year young boy who had had a serious stroke. He could not walk and was told he would never walk again. He went to the clinic and they worked with him. In 6 weeks of work, no drugs, he walked out under his own power. That is dramatic!

Many of the seniors I meet have become so depressed they just give up. I sit in many homes with auto accident victims and other terrible tragedies. A TV minister talks about how his mother was diagnosed with terminal cancer. Her attitude and lots of prayer and great doctors saved her and she has been cancer free for many years. I have experienced the ravages of cancer in my own mother and many friends. I recently buried a couple–both had it, and the wife went first. She had a great attitude right up till the end. I saw her the day before she passed and prayed with her. She still had a twinkle in her eye.

One of the best stories I have ever heard was from a lady years ago. She had been in a terrible auto accident and was in a coma. She heard the doctor tell her mother that she would either die or become a vegetable and never really recover. It made Linda so mad she started with all her might trying to focus and open her eyes and move her fingers. Within a few hours she opened her eyes and moved her hands. She got up in a few days and started rehab. Her anger motivated her. She went back to college and got her masters and teaches at a local college. She is not dead or a wheel chair bound victim. She is a vibrant teacher. What does that tell us?

For the person being taken care of, life can become traumatic and tragic. But their attitude can make all the difference in the world–recovery or just falling into a pit. One of the things I have observed is that some victims become angry and lash out–unfortunately hurting those closest to them. I have no idea what to do for that person except pray and try to get them to change their attitude. I have also read that life-threatening issues, like a heart attack or stroke or cancer or an accident, can change a person's personality. I have often seen the hopeless caretaker beaten down by an angry, unhappy patient. So what can we do to help them? Well, obviously pray because I believe prayer works, but encouragement can be a healer as well. I have shown videos from the Adaptive Training Foundation and videos of successful recoveries to discouraged people to show them a different way to view their circumstances. I believe good examples lead and challenge. Set an example yourself for that person who is hurting. Don't just tell them, show them. Be an example.

For the caretaker I have nothing but praise. It can be a terrible job, depending on the circumstances. Over the years as a Certified Senior Advisor I have made friends with great people who have caretaking agencies. Visiting Angels, Seniors Helping Seniors, and many other professional caretaking agencies, can be a great help. Don't be a martyr. Get some help and relief. Find a group of other caretakers to get together with and share stories and ideas. Do *not* let the patient lead you to isolate. I have seen that too many times where a devoted spouse is there twenty-four seven and burns out. Their health can begin to decline physically and mentally. Get exercise, get relief, take time off, and do not isolate. I had a customer many years ago who lived in a rural community outside Houston. His wife came down with Alzheimer's and cancer. He was so far out in the country that he was isolated to start with. He needed help, so I helped him with a reverse mortgage to provide some additional cash to pay for part time home health care. He needed to go to the grocery store and run errands. When I talked to him during the lending process I would update him then ask him questions about his life with his wife. I was sometimes on the phone for over an hour for what normally was a five-minute call. Even after the loan closed, we continued to talk on a weekly basis. Finally all the diseases took their toll and she passed away. I often thought it was a relief for him. They had no children and few friends and he chose not to have a memorial service. He just had a reception at his home for their few friends.

Throughout the ordeal I kept encouraging him and suggested he get a treadmill and some weights and exercise. I also suggested that he prepare the healthiest meals he could for both of them. He told me he lost weight, and the exercise was what kept him going. He told me when she was alive he would sleep in the same room and stay awake listening to make sure she was breathing. He was devoted to her and I know he greatly missed her, but he didn't stop taking care of himself during the process. That kept him going and I think it helped her too. I think when a patient sees their caretaker falling apart it hurts them as well. So if you are a caretaker: get help, exercise and stay connected. Don't isolate or lose connections. The stronger you stay the better you can take care of your patient and yourself.

There are many organizations that can help: Visiting Angels, Seniors Helping Seniors, The Council On Aging, and your local community outreach senior programs. See Power Tools (next chapter) for more. If you need help, ask for it! **ASK FOR HELP when you need it! Don't wait until you are pulling your hair out!**

From the veteran who was burned up, blown up, and beaten up, to the lady who got out of her coma one step at a time, I have witnessed many miracles–most because of *attitude* and *determination*. They talked *solution* and did the *planning* and *persevered* until the solution *happened!*

Power Tools

*A man's heart plans his way, but
the Lord directs his steps.*
Proverbs 16:9

I have written about having a plan and for me it is the cornerstone of success. How to make a plan? First of all you have to **write it down**. I believe a plan that isn't written down is just an idea–a thought–a wish. We don't need wishes. A plan requires action that writing empowers.

Planning anything requires some experienced advice. A friend's wife asked me for help to start a business making and selling hand-made greeting cards. I thought it was interesting to say the least. She had located a shop space and she had asked her husband for an investment of $250,000. I asked one question: how much experience did she have running a retail shop? None ... So the next question–had she any experience in the greeting card business? None ... So I advised she get a job in a

Hallmark gift card shop and learn about the business, first. Try it on, I suggested. You wouldn't buy a dress without trying it on to see if it fit you. It took about six weeks in the shop when Michael called me. She had left the shop, hated the business, and said it wasn't for her. That saved him a pretty penny and her a lot of time and effort.

Thinking about downsizing/rightsizing? Here are some ideas:

1. Find out what your home is worth, a realtor is your best source.
2. Where do you want to go? Why?
3. How are you going to pay for it? Do a Budget (example follows) and keep it current.
4. Who is your team? Realtor, title company, lender, insurance agent, etc.
5. Mover? Storage–is it needed?
6. Estate sale, donating needed?
7. Budget ... What will all this cost?
8. What is your fallback position?

Downsizing requires real planning, and *you* are the beneficiary of a good plan. What do you know–experientially–about what you want and how to get it? Plug the facts into the following tools.

Basic Plan

There are many different formats. My favorite planning tool is an outline:

1. **Goal:** What is your goal. What are you trying to achieve, stable retirement, financial security, good health, education, start a business, buy a toy; boat, etc., travel ... what is your goal?
2. **Financial:** What will it cost? Do a Budget and Financial Statement (examples following).
3. **Action Steps:** What action steps do you need to take? Save money, get job(s), downsize/rightsize, acquire education? What steps do you need to take? Example: Education–classes, degree plan; Business: Buy a franchise or start a business; Save Money: How much do you need? This is the most important step. Do your research and plan wise steps.

Basic Plan

4. **Schedule:** A plan must be timely. When do you do what. Example: Education, when do you go to a counselor, what classes to take and when. Write it all down. Seeing the print spurs further creativity.
5. **Legal:** What legal documents do you need? Trusts, Wills, Power of Attorney, Contracts. How does what you do affect you if you make a mistake? What legal protection do you and your family need?
6. **Conclusion:** What things need to change? Is the end result – your goal – likely to be achieved?

The crux of any plan is financial; so let's create a budget ...

Budget

Income: Social Security   _____

                Pension Income   _____

                Investment Income   _____

                Other Income   _____

                Total Income/month   _____

Expenses: Charity/Contributions   _____

                Mortgage/Rent   _____

                Taxes Real Estate   _____

                Insurance   _____

                Utilities (Electrical/Gas   _____

                Water/Sewer/Trash   _____

                Landscaping/Maint.   _____

                Car Payment   _____

                Home/Apt Insurance   _____

                Car Insurance   _____

                Health Insurance   _____

                HOA Dues   _____

                Credit Cards   _____

                Gas   _____

                Auto Maint.   _____

                Groceries   _____

                Entertainment   _____

                Other   _____

                Total Expenses/month   _____

Cash flow/month (Income – Expenses)   _____

Looking at these facts helps focus on what you CAN change before it's too late. Changes that IMPROVE your cash flow. What you are spending tells the tale of your situation. A hard look at your financial situation can be difficult, but an eye opener ...

Financial Statement

Assets:

    Home   _____

    Cash - Bank Accts   _____

    Investments   _____

    Cash Surrender Life Ins   _____

        Total Assets   _____

Liabilities:

    Car   _____

    Home   _____

    Credit/Debt   _____

    Other   _____

        Total Liabilities   _____

Net Worth (Assets - Liabilities)   _____

Challenges of Change

Now take a look down the road at where you could be. What happens if your income is cut, unexpectedly? When one member of a family passes away, the lesser of the Social Security checks goes away, too. This can be devastating. Therefore, looking down the road at what your income and expenses CAN be is the best way to CHALLENGE CHANGE. My wife's friend (very good with money) says the more you "play" with the numbers, the more you accumulate because you know intimately where you REALLY are and take the action(s) necessary.

Conclusion

¹³ Brethren, I do not count myself to have apprehended; but one thing I do, forgetting those things which are behind and reaching forward to those things which are ahead, ¹⁴ I press toward the goal for the prize of the upward call of God in Christ Jesus.
Philippians 3:13-14

Most of us think of retirement as taking it easy. It isn't, and we need NOT to retire but to *move forward* and do what we need to *stay connected* and *keep learning* from others. We are designed for interaction and communication. That has been proven with study after study. So press on to enjoying others and stop being afraid. Stay in touch with those you trust. Stay savvy about as much technology as you can. Use it to communicate. Be wise. If you are afraid of being hacked, don't open or link to anything you aren't sure of. Get training in things that interest you. I frequently see a generation gap in technology. Most senior centers have computer classes that are fun – a good place to **meet others who**

are also staying active and are life-long learners. Do whatever it takes to stay active in heart, mind, and body. When I die I want a real party with lots of good food and wine and laughter. I want stories about my crazy experiences and how I lived my life. I want everyone to come and have a ball celebrating my life. I don't want a half-empty church with no one remembering how much fun we had. I love to cook, I love being on the radio, I love my job, I love my church family, I love my family, and I love life. Try it–it's the best!

We have walked through a few stories about helping seniors and living life. I challenge you to rewrite your story today and get excited about living. I would love to hear of your new adventure(s). Every year I find more to do ...

and more I *cannot* do. Age has a way of doing that to all of us. However, I enjoy life now more than ever before –my sense of humor helps, of course. Everyone has limitations, but let's make adjustments, keep life interesting, and keep moving forward. I think life is just one big learning curve and every day presents new chances to **CHALLENGE CHANGE!**

Jim Blythe, CSA

JimBlythe.net   214 502 4600
NMLS 311548   JamBly163@yahoo.com

Resources

National:

Society of Certified Senior Advisors: People throughout the US who have passed extensive background checks and coursework regarding aging issues – locator at www.csa.us under Resources

Visiting Angels: http://www.visitingangels.com/ – non-medical senior home care services

Seniors Helping Seniors: http://www.seniorshelpingseniors.com/ – senior care by seniors

Care Patrol: http://carepatrol.com/ – residential housing locators

Disabled American Veterans: https://www.dav.org/– lifetime of support for veterans of all generations and their families

Texas:

Veterans County Service Officer: http://www.vcsoat.org/page-1494040–Counties in Texas with populations over 250,000 has a designated Veterans County Service officer who helps all veterans fill out paperwork for free

Dallas:

Senior Centers: http://www.dallascounty.org/department/hhs/seniorcenters.html

Dallas Veterans County Service Officer: James Henderson–http://www.dallascounty.org/department/veterans/james.php

Resources

Red Book/Council on Aging:

North Central Texas Area Agency on Aging
Benefits Enrollment Center, Reverse Mortgage Default Assistance BEC
616 Six Flags Drive
Arlington, TX 76011
(800) 272-3921
http://www.nctcog.org/cs/aging/index.asp
Blue Book: http://www.seniorsbluebook.com

Forgiveness:

www.ForgivingForward.com - Bruce & Toni Hebel share the protocols of forgiveness – must do *AND* how to!

www.ingramcontent.com/pod-product-compliance
Ingram Content Group UK Ltd.
Pitfield, Milton Keynes, MK11 3LW, UK
UKHW041949230426
12048UKWH00008B/226